W9-COH-028

DATE DUE			

SMILE-A-WHILE

RIDDLES

By Gary Chmielewski
Drawings by Ron G. Clark

Library of Congress Cataloging in Publication Data

Chmielewski, Gary, 1946-
  Riddles.

  (Smile-a-while joke book)
  Summary: A collection of gentle riddles such as "How do you make an egg roll? Push it down the hill."
  1. Riddles, Juvenile. [1. Riddles] I. Title.
II. Series.
PN6371.5.C45 1986   818'.5402   86-17720
ISBN 0-86592-686-7

ROURKE ENTERPRISES, INC.
VERO BEACH, FLORIDA 32964

How do you make an egg roll?
Push it down the hill.

Why is electricity so dangerous?
It doesn't know how to conduct itself.

Why was the wheel such an important invention?
It got everything else going.

What is the deepest part of the Pacific Ocean?
The bottom.

What kind of umbrella does Superman carry on a rainy day?
A wet one.

Why is an old car like a baby?
They both have a rattle.

What bird is at your meal?
A swallow.

Three fat men were walking under one small umbrella, but none got wet. Why?
It wasn't raining.

When is it proper to serve milk in a saucer?
When you feed a cat.

What did the mayonnaise say to the refrigerator?
"Close the door. Can't you see I'm dressing?"

Why did Christy go outside with her purse open?
She heard there would be some change in the weather.

When is a mystery writer like a vegetable farmer?
When he digs up a plot.

Why should potatoes act better than other vegetables?
They have eyes to see what they are doing.

What did the corn stalk say to the farmer?
"Stop picking on me!"

Where do children grow?
In a kindergarten

Why are flowers lazy?
Because you always find them in beds.

What time is it when a clock strikes 13?
Time to get it fixed.

When can you carry water in a strainer?
When it is frozen.

What song does a tea kettle sing?
"Home on the Range."

What are the smartest animals in the sea?
Fish. They go around in schools.

Why did the mother knit three socks for her son?
He grew another foot over the winter.

When do one and one not make two?
When they make 11.

When the apple wanted to fight the banana, why did the banana run away?
Because it was yellow.

Some months have thirty days. Some months have thirty-one days. How many months have twenty-eight days?
All of them.

Why do bees hum?
Because they don't know the words.

What did the big firecracker say to the little firecracker?
"My pop is bigger than your pop!"

If you lived in a cemetery, with what would you open the gate?
A skeleton key.

What is the tallest building in your city?
The library — it has the most stories.

How do monsters count to fifteen?
They use their fingers.

What did the ocean say when the plane flew over?
Nothing it just waved.

How is a book like a tree?
They both have leaves.

What country can't get enough to eat?
Hungary.

What country helps you to cook?
Greece.

How do you know an elephant will stay for a long time when it comes to visit?
It brings its trunk.

Why is Santa Claus like the Farmer-in-the-Dell?
They both like to hoe, hoe, hoe.

Why did Robin Hood only steal from the rich to give to the poor?
It wouldn't have worked the other way.

Why does an Indian wear feathers?
To keep his wigwarm/'wig warm'.

What is black and white and has sixteen wheels?
A zebra on roller skates.

Why does a spider make a good baseball player?
Because it catches flies.

Why did the boy put on a wet shirt and pants?
The label said "wash and wear".

Where was the Magna Carta signed?
At the bottom.

In what battle did General Wolfe cry, "I die happy"?
His last one!

What kind of dog does a person bite?
A hot dog!

Why did the fireman wear red suspenders?
To keep his pants up.
Why did the fireman wear blue suspenders?
Because he couldn't find his red ones.

Why does a dog wag its tail?
Because no one else will wag it for him.

Which moves faster — hot or cold?
Hot. Anybody can catch a cold.

What tree can you carry in your hand?
Palm.

What kind of candy bar can you find in outer space?
Milky Way.

How many hamburgers can you eat on an empty stomach?
One. After that your stomach is no longer empty.

Why is a rabbit's nose always so shiny?
Because its powder puff is on the wrong end.

What goes all the way from New York to Chicago without moving?
Railroad tracks.

Why is watermelon filled with water?
It's planted in the spring.

What did the rug say to the floor?
"Don't move. I have you covered!"

Why did the worker sit on a clock?
He wanted to work overtime.

What do you call a cat who drinks lemonade?
A sour puss.

Why did the boy throw the clock off the roof?
He wanted to see time fly.

How much dirt can you take out of a hole three feet, three feet by two feet?
None. The dirt has already been taken out.

What are the largest ants in the world?
Gi-ants.

How much water can you put in an empty glass?
None. It wouldn't be empty.

If a king sits on gold, who sits on silver?
The Lone Ranger.